Celtic Cuisine

Celtic Cuisine
Published in Great Britain in 2023 by Graffeg Limited.

Written by Gilli Davies copyright © 2023.
Food photography by Huw Jones copyright
© 2023. Food Styling by Paul Lane.
Post Production by Matt Braham.
Designed and produced by Graffeg Limited
copyright © 2023.

Landscape photographs © Shutterstock pages:
8-9, 30-31, 56-57, 82-83, 104-105, 118-119, 140-141.

Graffeg Limited, 24 Stradey Park Business
Centre, Mwrwg Road, Llangennech, Llanelli,
Carmarthenshire, SA14 8YP, Wales, UK.
Tel 01554 824000. www.graffeg.com

The publisher acknowledges the financial support
of the Books Council of Wales. www.gwales.com

ISBN 9781802584448

Printed in China TT14022023

1 2 3 4 5 6 7 8 9

Recipes from Ireland, Scotland, Wales, Cornwall, Isle of Man, Brittany and Galicia by Gilli Davies and Huw Jones.

Celtic Cuisine

GRAFFEG

Contents

Introduction

Gathering recipes for this Celtic cookery book has been a stimulating experience, highlighting a common thread of cookery skills, ingredients and culinary traditions throughout the Celtic countries of Scotland, Ireland, Wales, the Isle of Man, Cornwall, Brittany in northwest France and Galicia in northwest Spain.

Traditionally, the Celts cooked over an open fire, with a large pot suspended over the glowing coals to make soups and stews. This is hardly a style of cooking that suits us today, however, the griddle, a cookery implement that has stood the test of time, is still very much used in many of the Celtic regions. At one time bread was baked slowly on the griddle by the Celts, but today it is used mainly for cooking a variety of pancakes. In Brittany these are still the thin, crisp crêpes, but elsewhere you might well find potato cakes in Ireland, oatcakes in Scotland and Welsh cakes in Wales, and it is of interest to see how the regional variations have developed.

The ingredients in these regions are some of the finest possible. With excellent and unspoilt coastlines, the fish, shellfish and sea vegetables are plentiful. Inland, the rivers sport good fish too, and the Celts, being good stockmen, have always bred the finest breeds of cattle, pigs and sheep. Wild deer and other game are still plentiful, and the hedgerows, moors and open spaces harbour a myriad of exciting, untamed ingredients to add flavours of berries, blossoms, fungi and herbs.

The Celts have deep roots in European history and can be traced back to 500 BC. They have been one of the greatest peoples and were established across a vast area from Britain and Ireland in the north to Spain and France in the south, spreading east to southern

Germany, the Alps, Bohemia and later Italy, the Balkans and even central Turkey. First identified in Switzerland and known as the Celts of La Tène, history shows how they shared many common bonds of language, customs, art and culture. Known in France as Gauls and Galatae to the Greeks, it was the Romans with their conquering armies who drove the Celts north and by AD 43 the Roman Emperor Claudius had worked his way up to the Highlands of Scotland, which was then known as Caledonia. In fact, Ireland was the only part of the Celtic world to escape Rome.

Although the Romans failed to conquer Galicia, the early Bretons did succumb and it was later in the 6th century that a resurgence in Celtic culture took western Britons across the channel to establish Brittany. However, the Celtic revival of the early Middle Ages was halted by the Vikings, with subsequent centuries experiencing a weakening of the Celts' identity, culture and language. It was due to the emergence of vigorous nationalist movements in the last century that today Celtic tongues are spoken in most of the Celtic regions and a sense of shared culture has developed within art, music and, of course, cooking.

Oats were once the staple of all the northern regions, but today buckwheat is favoured in Brittany in pancakes, while potatoes major in Ireland and wheat is the most common grain used in Wales. Regional variations in the names of ingredients change too, as with the spring onion, which is known as a scallion in Ireland, gibbons in Wales and syboes in Scotland.

Cookery does not stand still though and recipes develop with every generation of cook in the kitchen. This cookbook therefore covers a range of recipes from the traditional dishes rooted in the Celtic past to modern interpretations of old-fashioned recipes. I hope you enjoy them all.

Gilli Davies

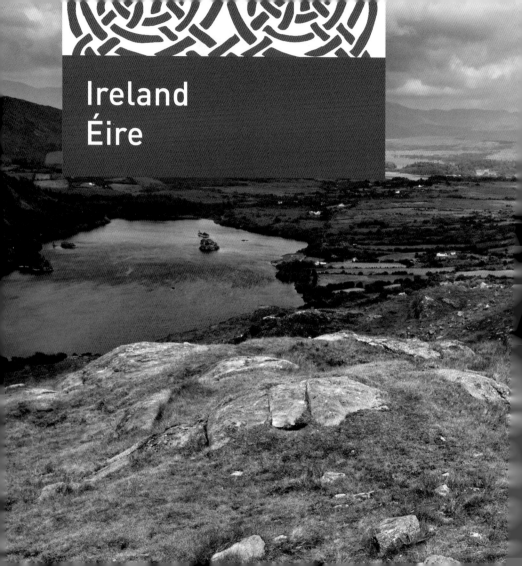

Ireland
Éire

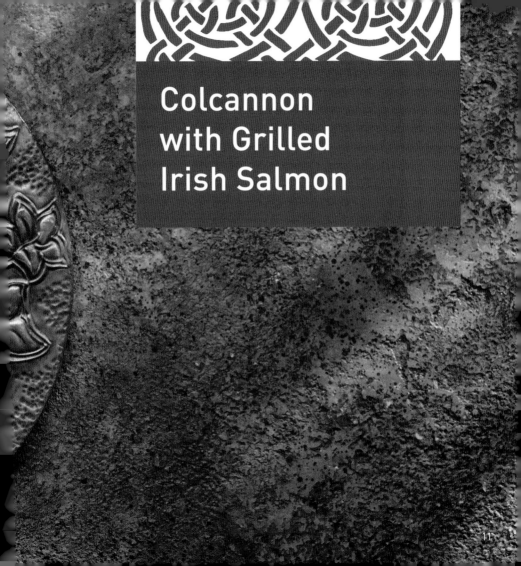

Colcannon
with Grilled
Irish Salmon

Colcannon with Grilled Irish Salmon

The name colcannon comes from the Gaelic *cál* and *caineann*, which translates to kale and spring onion.

Any cabbage works well instead of kale, and finely chopped leeks can be used instead of springs onions too.

Colcannon has been traditionally served at Halloween with coins or small charms wrapped in foil hidden in the mash. Finding a button meant you would remain a bachelor, a thimble meant you would remain a spinster for the coming year, a ring meant you would get married and a coin meant you would come into wealth.

Ingredients

1kg floury potatoes, peeled

6 spring onions, sliced

200g curly kale or green cabbage, washed and finely chopped

100g butter

Salt

Black pepper

100ml whole milk or single cream

Serves 4

Method

1 Cut the potatoes into even-sized chunks and boil in salted boiling water until soft, around 15–20 minutes.

2 Melt the butter in a large frying pan and cook the spring onions for two minutes before adding the shredded kale. It seems like a lot, but it will soon wilt as you stir.

3 Drain the cooked potatoes and mash well to a smooth texture.

4 Stir in the cooked kale with the spring onions and all the buttery juices.

5 Season well and add the milk or cream until the texture is firm and creamy.

Grilled Salmon

Ingredients

4 x 175-200g pieces thick salmon fillet, skinned

50g butter, melted

Salt and freshly ground black pepper

Serves 4

Method

1 Brush the salmon on all sides with melted butter and season well.

2 Place on a lightly buttered baking tray and grill for 8 minutes until just cooked through.

3 Serve the grilled salmon with the colcannon.

Boxty Potato Pancakes with Full Irish Breakfast

Boxty Potato Pancakes with Full Irish Breakfast

Boxty is an authentic Irish dish which originated in the 1700s. Ireland was a poor country then, with a large majority of Irish people relying on the potato harvest for their staple diet, so the potato famine of 1845-1852 struck a devastating blow to the population.

The name boxty probably comes from the Irish *arán bocht tí*, meaning 'poor-house bread'. The recipe is a combination of raw and cooked potato, setting it apart from other types of potato pancakes or scones.

An old Irish rhyme goes: 'Boxty on the griddle, boxty in the pan; if you can't make boxty, you'll never get a man.'

A hearty breakfast would originally have sustained a farmer for a day's work in the fields and all the ingredients might well have come from the farm, but today you could expect to find any or all of the following on the menu:

Bacon rashers
Sausages
Fried eggs
Black or white pudding
Mushrooms
Tomatoes
Baked beans
Soda bread

Ingredients

Boxty Pancakes

225g mashed potatoes

225g raw potato, grated

250g plain flour

1 teaspoon baking powder

Good pinch salt

225ml buttermilk (or more if needed)

Butter, for the griddle

Serves 4-6

···

Method

1 In a large mixing bowl, combine the mashed potatoes with the grated raw potato, then add the flour, baking powder and salt and mix well.

2 Slowly add the buttermilk and stir gently, but don't overmix. The mixture should be like a very firm, thick batter, almost like a dough.

3 Heat a griddle or non-stick frying pan over medium heat and add a little butter, then spoon some of the boxty batter into the pan.

4 Flatten and shape into a round pancake shape and fry until golden brown on the bottom.

5 Turn and continue to cook until golden brown on top too, turning the heat down if they are browning too quickly (remember there are raw potatoes which need to cook).

6 Continue to add a little butter and fry the boxty until all the batter is finished. Serve hot.

Irish Stew

A Celtic classic, Irish stew would have originally been made in a large metal pot suspended over the glowing embers of an open fire. Mutton was the dominant ingredient because sheep were reared for their wool and milk, so only the older animals ended up in the cooking pot, needing a long, slow cook.

Irish Stew

Ingredients

2 tablespoons oil

3 large onions, peeled and thickly sliced

1kg (about 8-10 medium-sized) floury potatoes

1kg stewing mutton or neck of lamb, cut into thick slices

2 sprigs fresh thyme

Chopped parsley or chives, to serve

Serves 4-6

....

Method

1 Heat the oven to 160°C/140°C Fan/Gas 3.

2 Heat the oil in a large casserole dish over a medium flame and cook the onions gently until soft and golden, but not browned.

3 Remove from the casserole dish and set aside.

4 Peel and slice half of the potatoes thinly and arrange as a layer in the base of the casserole dish, then top with the fried onions, lamb and thyme. Season generously and pour in 850ml cold water. Bring to a bare simmer, then cover and transfer the casserole to the oven for 2 hours.

5 Check that there is still enough water to cover, add more if necessary. Peel and slice the remaining potatoes and arrange across the top of the meat. Leave the lid off the casserole dish and return to the oven for another hour.

6 Serve the Irish stew with fresh green vegetables and maybe a chunk of soda bread to soak up the gravy.

When I learnt to make traditional Irish stew while living in Northern Ireland in the 1970s in quite a sophisticated café, the recipe had just five simple ingredients: mutton, potatoes, onions, seasoning and water.

It was delicious, nourishing and very filling. These days, lamb often replaces mutton for a more delicate version, and some cooks add carrots, turnips, thyme and even pearl barley. As you can tell, it's a very flexible dish.

Irish Soda Bread

Irish Soda Bread

Irish soda bread may be made with white or wholemeal flour, depending on where you are in Ireland. In Northern Ireland brown soda bread is commonly known as wheaten bread.

The reason this sort of loaf is called soda bread is because the bread rises with a combination of bicarbonate of soda mixed with acidic buttermilk.

There are many advantages to making this classic Irish bread. It's very easy to prepare, quick to bake and delicious. This is an authentic recipe from the turn of the last century.

Ingredients

425g wholemeal flour

125g plain white flour

75g butter

1 teaspoon salt

Pinch sugar

1 teaspoon bicarbonate of soda

300ml buttermilk or fresh milk soured with 1 teaspoon of lemon juice

25g sunflower seeds (optional)

Makes 1 loaf

Method

1 Preheat the oven to 200°C/180°C Fan/Gas 6.

2 Mix all the dry ingredients together in a large bowl.

3 Rub in the butter until the mixture resembles fine breadcrumbs.

4 Make a well in the centre and add
the buttermilk.

5 Shape into a round cake and
sprinkle with sunflower seeds.

6 Bake for 35-40 minutes.

It's generally not a loaf to keep, so
best baked in small batches and
eaten fresh with butter and a good
selection of Irish cheeses. Look out
for Gubbeen, Cashel Blue, Killeen
Goat, Cnoc Dubh, Knockanore
Smoked, Cais Na Tire, Wicklow Blue
and Coolea amongst many others
now available.

Barmbrack

This traditional Irish fruit bread is very similar to tea breads found in most Celtic countries. Modern versions are raised by self-raising flour, but this is a traditional recipe using fresh yeast.

Barmbrack

Ingredients

450g strong bread flour

1 teaspoon salt

25g butter

5 tablespoons caster sugar

1 egg, beaten

Pinch cinnamon or mixed spice

225g sultanas and currants, mixed

25g mixed peel, chopped

Warm honey, to glaze

For the yeast starter solution

300ml warm milk

1 teaspoon caster sugar

25g fresh yeast or dried equivalent

Makes 1 loaf

Method

1 Line the bottom of a 900g loaf tin with buttered greaseproof paper.

2 Prepare the starter solution: dissolve the sugar in the milk and add the yeast. Leave in a warm place for a few minutes.

3 Sieve the flour and salt into a bowl. Rub the butter into the flour and add the sugar. Stir in the cinnamon, sultanas, currants and peel.

4 Add the yeast solution and the beaten egg to the flour mixture and work to a stiff dough. Knead well for a few minutes.

5 Place the dough in the loaf tin. Cover and leave in a warm place for 1 hour to rise.

6 Preheat the oven to 220°C/200°C Fan/Gas 7.

7 Remove the cover and bake the brack for 5 minutes in the hot oven, then reduce the heart to 180°C/160°C Fan/ Gas 4 and continue to bake for another 45 minutes until golden and cooked through. Cool on a rack and brush with warm honey to glaze.

Scotland
Alba

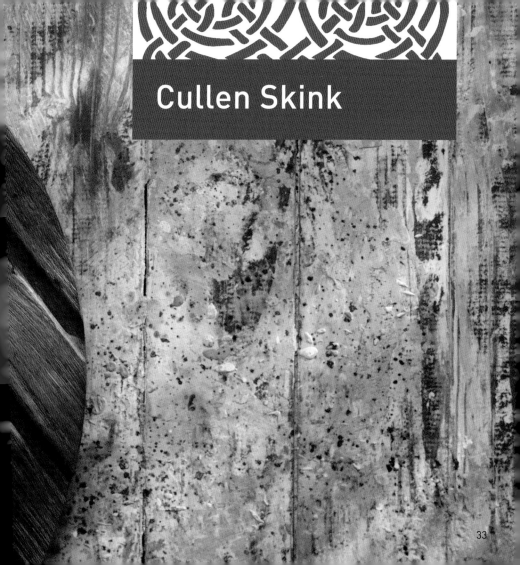

Cullen Skink

Cullen Skink

Cullen skink is a thick Scottish soup made from smoked haddock, potatoes and onions or leeks. An authentic Cullen skink will use finnan haddie, but it may be prepared with any other smoked haddock, undyed for preference. This soup is a local speciality from the town of Cullen in Moray, on the northeast coast of Scotland.

Originally, Cullen skink was a type of beef broth made from the front legs of cattle, and the word skink was used to mean a shin or knuckle of beef. Around the early 1890s smoked haddock was in a much more plentiful supply than beef around the area of Cullen, as the village had become specialist in producing it, and so it was used to make a simple smoked fish soup instead.

Ingredients

500g smoked haddock, skin on

1 bay leaf

25g butter

1 onion, peeled and finely chopped

1 leek, washed and cut into chunks

2 medium potatoes, peeled and cut into chunks

350ml whole milk

150ml single cream

Chives and parsley, chopped, to serve

Serves 6

Method

1 Put the fish and bay leaf into a pan and cover with about 300ml cold water. Bring gently to the boil, then take off the heat, cover the pan and leave to cool.

2 Melt the butter in another large pan on a medium-low heat and add the onion. Cook the onion gently for two minutes, then add the leek and continue cooking to soften without colouring for about 10 minutes.

3 Stir in the potato chunks. Pour in the haddock cooking liquid and bay leaf, season with black pepper and bring to a simmer. Cook until the potato is soft.

4 Meanwhile, remove the skin and any bones from the haddock and break into largish flakes.

5 Add the fish to the pan with the milk and cream and heat through.

6 Season to taste and serve with a sprinkling of chopped parsley and chives on top.

Mince 'n' Tatties
with Skirlie

A warming and hearty Scottish classic, mince and tatties is a much-loved family dish for many Scots. A survey in 2009 found that it was the most popular Scottish dish, with a third of respondents saying that they eat mince and tatties once a week.

Mince 'n' Tatties with Skirlie

Ingredients

500g minced Scotch beef

1 onion, peeled and diced

2 medium carrots, peeled and diced

1 small stick celery, diced

1 tablespoon vegetable oil

2 tablespoons plain flour

600ml beef stock

2 tablespoons Worcestershire sauce

Freshly ground black pepper and salt

Serves 4

Method

1 Heat the oil in a large frying pan over a medium heat, add the diced vegetables and cook for about 5 minutes until softened but not brown, then increase the heat, add the meat to the pan and fry until it is well browned, about 8-10 minutes.

2 When the meat is browned, slightly reduce the heat then sprinkle the flour over the meat and vegetables and stir for a couple of minutes to cook the flour.

3 Add the stock, Worcestershire sauce, salt and pepper. Stir while the sauce comes gently to the boil and begins to thicken.

4 Cover the pan and simmer for about 30 minutes, adding more stock as necessary, until everything is tender.

5 Serve the mince in shallow bowls with buttered mash and skirlie.

Skirlie

Ingredients

100g medium or pinhead oatmeal

50g beef or pork dripping,
or 1 tablespoon oil

1 small onion, peeled and chopped

Pinch of salt

Water as needed

Serves 4

....

Method

1 Melt the fat in a small frying pan over gentle heat and fry the onions until they begin to brown, then add the oats and cook until all the fat has been absorbed.

2 Continue to cook for another minute or two until they smell like toast, then add a tablespoon or two of water and a pinch of salt. When the water has disappeared, taste the oats. If they taste good to you, the skirlie is ready.

You can always add more water and cook for a bit longer. Keep on doing this until the oats are cooked – the skirlie should be quite dry, with no residual water sitting around.

Casserole of Scottish Wild Venison in Red Wine

Casserole of Scottish Wild Venison in Red Wine

Venison comes from the four species of wild deer found in Scotland: roe deer, red deer, sika deer and fallow deer.

The red deer is the largest native land mammal in the UK and is found predominantly in the open hill range, characteristic of much of upland Scotland, but also using woodlands and plantations, particularly for shelter.

Wild deer need to be managed to maintain a healthy population in balance with their habitat and the land use of the area where they live. 'Taking' of wild deer is governed by open and close seasons that are different for each species and each sex. However, because of these differences, and also because deer that damage crops and forestry can legally be shot out of season under a General License, it is possible for wild venison to be sourced all year round.

Ingredients

1kg stewing venison, cut into 2.5cm cubes

300ml red wine

2 bay leaves

1 tablespoon oil

25g butter

1 large onion, peeled and chopped

25g flour

300ml game or chicken stock

1 tablespoon redcurrant jelly

175g button mushrooms, sliced

Salt and freshly ground black pepper

Serves 4

Method

1 Heat the oven to 150°C/130°C Fan/ Gas 3.

2 Place the chopped venison in a bowl with the red wine and bay leaves, cover and leave to marinate in the fridge for 48 hours. Strain the red wine and reserve, discarding the bay leaves.

3 Heat the oil and butter in a casserole dish and gently sauté the onion for ten minutes, then stir in the flour and continue to cook for about another minute.

4 Slowly blend in the wine and stock and bring to the boil, stirring until thickened. Stir in the venison, redcurrant jelly and seasoning. Cover and boil for another 5 minutes. Reduce the heat, then simmer in a slow oven for about 4 hours, or until tender.

5 Add the mushrooms for the last 30 minutes or so.

6 Serve with mashed or new boiled potatoes and green vegetables.

Venison comes from the four species of wild deer found in Scotland: roe deer, red deer, sika deer and fallow deer.

Haggis with Neeps and Tatties

Haggis with Neeps and Tatties

Haggis is a tradtional Scottish dish containing sheep's offal (heart, liver and lungs), minced with onion, oatmeal, suet, spices, and salt, mixed with stock, and traditionally simmered in the animal's stomach for approximately three hours (although nowadays haggis tends to be simmered in a casing rather than the stomach). It is often considered to be the national dish of Scotland and is memorialised in Robert Burns' poem 'Address to a Haggis'.

Originally a modest dish ensuring no part of the sheep goes to waste, haggis can now be found on the menu in most pubs and many restaurants, where one can encounter it in anything from filo pastry with Drambuie sauce, to the haggis, neeps and tatties roulade on sale at the Scottish Parliament's Holyrood café. Furthermore, some supermarkets have been known to sell products which are not sheep based. This is very wrong! A vegetarian version is now also available and while still 'wrong', is quite tasty! Haggis is traditionally served with mashed neeps (turnips) and mashed tatties (potatoes).

Ingredients

500g haggis, ready made

1kg potatoes, such as Maris Piper, cut into similar-sized pieces

100ml milk

150g unsalted butter

1 swede, peeled and diced

2 large carrots, diced

Serves 4

Method

1 Heat the haggis, following pack instructions. When the haggis has 30 minutes cooking time remaining, tip the potatoes into a large pan of generously salted cold water, then bring to boil over a medium heat and cook for 10-12 minutes until very tender when

pierced with a fork. Drain well and leave to steam dry in the colander for 10 minutes.

2 Add half the milk and two-thirds of the butter to the pan used to cook the potatoes and warm over a low heat until the butter is melted and the milk is just steaming. Remove from the heat and return the potatoes to a pan, then use a potato masher to mash everything together. Season well with salt and pepper.

3 Meanwhile, cook the swede and carrots in a pan of boiling water for 18-20 minutes until very tender when pierced with a fork. Drain well and leave to steam dry in the colander for 10 minutes. Return the vegetables to the pan along with the remaining milk and butter, then coarsely mash using a potato masher, leaving a roughish texture. Season well.

4 Serve the haggis with the neeps and tatties alongside.

While it is eaten all year round, haggis is particularly associated with Burns Night, when it is traditionally served with 'neeps and tatties' (Scots: swede, yellow turnip or rutabaga and potatoes, boiled and mashed separately) and a 'dram' (i.e. a glass of Scotch whisky).

Mashed together, neeps and tatties is also known as 'clapshot'.

Scottish
Shortbread

Mary, Queen of Scots is often credited with the invention, or at least refinement, of modern shortbread, as it was the cooks at her court who further improved it by taking influences from French cooking and refining the biscuit using butter, flour and sugar as the main ingredients.

Scottish Shortbread

Ingredients

225g butter

100g caster sugar

250g plain flour

75g cornflour

Sugar, to sprinkle

Serves 4

Method

1 Heat the oven to bake at 180°C/160°C Fan/Gas 4.

2 Cream the butter and sugar together in a bowl.

3 Gradually add the flour and cornflour and mix to form a dough.

4 Either grease or line a 30 x 20cm baking tin.

5 Press the shortbread mixture into the pan and prick with a fork.

6 Bake for 15-20 minutes, or until pale golden brown.

7 While still warm, sprinkle with sugar and cut into portions.

The term 'short' refers
to the crumbly texture
from the large quantity of
butter.

Scottish
Cranachan

Scottish Cranachan

Ingredients

50g medium or pinhead oatmeal

300ml double cream

2 tablespoons runny heather honey

2 tablespoons whisky

225g raspberries

Serves 4

Method

1 Heat a frying pan gently and toast the oatmeal lightly. Alternatively, spread the oatmeal over a baking tray and grill gently until light brown.

2 Whisk the cream until it holds its shape but is not stiff.

3 Add the honey and whisky.

4 Fold the cooled oatmeal gently into the cream.

5 Arrange layers of the oatmeal mixture with the fresh raspberries in tall glasses.

6 Serve at once to enjoy the crunchy, nutty flavour of the oats.

This is a recipe from my grandmother, Ethel Miln, who served it to her family in the 1930s. It is still popular today and can be adapted to serve with other fresh fruit, although Scottish raspberries are particularly good. It is similar to Welsh *llymry*.

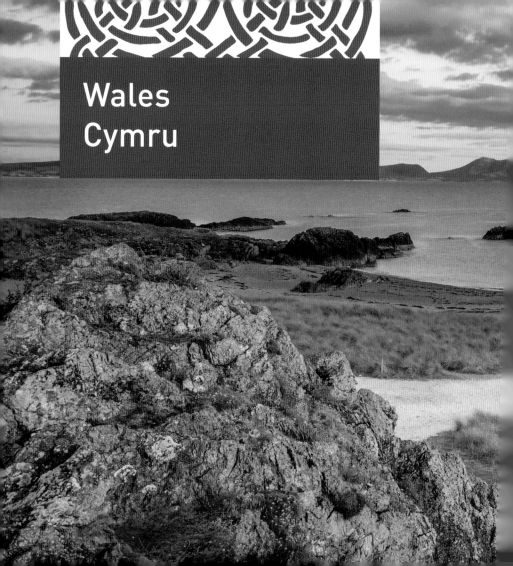

Wales
Cymru

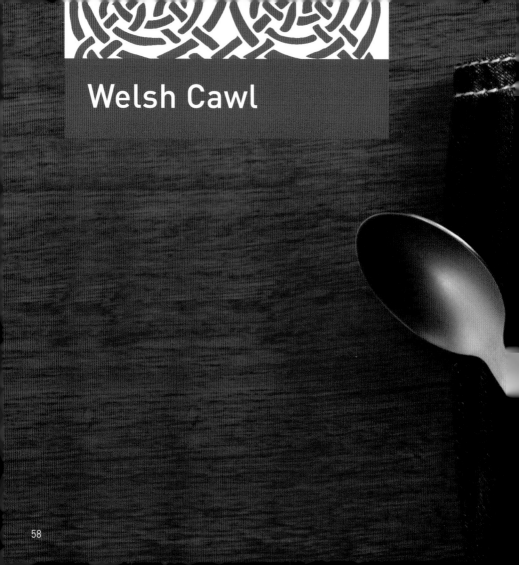

Welsh Cawl

Welsh Cawl

Ingredients

1kg bacon or ham, shoulder
or corner

1 onion

1 carrot

1 parsnip

1 bay leaf

Bunch parsley, stems and tops used
separately

25g butter

1 large leek, white and green part
separated and diced

3 carrots, peeled and cubed

2 parsnips, peeled and cubed

2 turnips, peeled and cubed

Bunch fresh winter savory or sage

Salt and pepper

Serves 4-6

Method

1 Soak the bacon or ham for a couple
of hours in cold water to remove some
of the salt.

2 Rinse well and place in a large pan
with enough cold water to cover.

3 Add the whole onion, carrot,
parsnip, bay leaf and parsley stalks.

4 Simmer gently for an hour, then
leave to cool before skimming the fat
from the surface.

5 Remove the bacon from the stock,
strain the liquid and retain for later.

6 Take some slices from the bacon
and set aside for another meal before
cutting the remainder into chunks for
the cawl.

7 Melt the butter in a large, clean
pan and gently fry the cubed carrots,
parsnips, turnips and white portion of
the leek for 5 minutes.

8 Pour on the reserved stock, add the chunks of bacon and the chopped parsley, savory and green leek.

9 Simmer for a further 20 minutes.

10 Season well and serve the cawl with chunks of fresh bread.

Although most cawl prepared in Wales today is made with lamb, in the past a pot of cawl might have been made from bacon that had been hanging on a hook in the kitchen to cure during the cold winter months. With root vegetables and herbs from the garden, it would have been the mainstay meal for many rural families.

Welsh Rarebit

Welsh Rarebit

Ingredients

225g strong-flavoured cheddar cheese

25g butter, melted

1 tablespoon Worcestershire sauce

1 tablespoon mustard

1 tablespoon flour

4 tablespoons beer

4 slices bread

Cayenne pepper, to garnish

Serves 4

Method

1 Toast the bread on one side only.

2 Grate the cheese and mix with the other ingredients to form a firm paste.

3 Spread the cheese mixture over the untoasted sides of the toast.

4 Grill gently until the topping is cooked through, bubbling and golden brown.

Perhaps this is the most famous of all Welsh recipes. Always a favourite in Wales, and known as 'roasted cheese' in medieval times, Welsh rarebit has not always been a rich savoury dish. It was once a recipe for using tough, poor-quality cheese, at a time when the cream from the top of the milk was used for making butter, leaving only the skimmed milk for cheesemaking.

Today, Welsh rarebit can be prepared with one of the many cheddar-type Welsh cheeses, which are full of flavour.

Glamorgan
Sausages

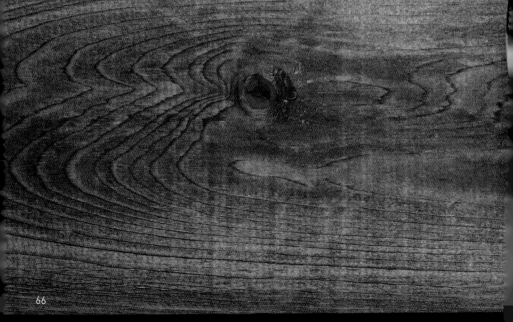

Glamorgan Sausages

Ingredients

150g fresh breadcrumbs

1 small leek, finely chopped

2 tablespoons laverbread (or pureed spinach)

75g Caerphilly cheese, grated

1 tablespoon fresh parsley, chopped

Salt and freshly ground black pepper

Pinch dry mustard

2 eggs, beaten

2 tablespoons light cooking oil

Makes 12

Method

1 Mix together the breadcrumbs, leek, laverbread, cheese, parsley, seasoning and mustard.

2 Use the beaten eggs to bind the mixture together.

3 Divide into 12 portions and form into sausage shapes.

4 Fry the Glamorgan sausages in the oil until crisp and golden brown on all sides.

Wales's answer to the vegetarian sausage, these are named after Glamorgan cheese which was made from the milk of Glamorgan cows. Though this is no longer made, any good Caerphilly cheese will work well.

As for the laverbread seaweed, which is a favourite in south Wales, you can use spinach as an alternative.

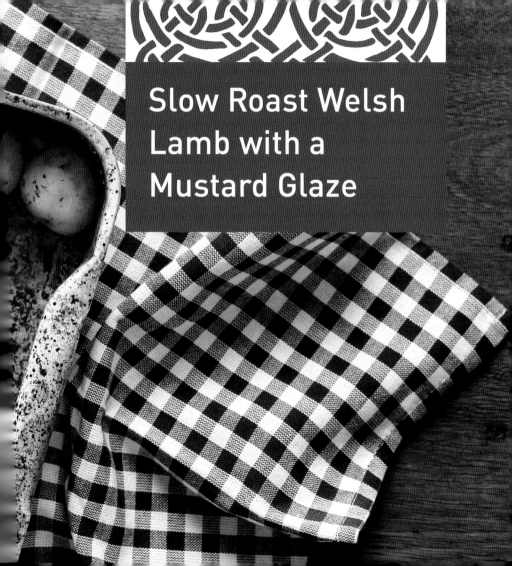

Slow Roast Welsh Lamb with a Mustard Glaze

Slow Roast Welsh Lamb with a Mustard Glaze

Ingredients

3kg lamb, shoulder or leg

6 tablespoons mustard

1 tablespoon cayenne pepper

5 tablespoons light muscovado sugar

1 tablespoon salt

1 tablespoon vegetable oil

Serves 4

Method

1 Remove the bone from the lamb if you want to make the carving process easier.

2 Mix the mustard, pepper, sugar, salt and oil together.

3 Pour over the lamb and leave to marinade for at least 2 hours in the fridge.

4 Cook at 180°C/350°F/Gas 4 for 3-4 hours, basting with the juices at times and turning the meat over after a couple of hours.

5 Cut the lamb into slices and serve with a mixture of seasonal vegetables, or, for a family meal in the garden, just fold slices of the lamb into fresh baps.

'Sunday morning and the house is full of good smells, promises of things to come. Roast lamb, smothered in sweet spices and herbs, smells even better than most, and the flavour lives up to expectations! Butter was added to it, brown sugar, ginger and maybe something else. In a short time I was as warm as toast and glowing with geniality'. From *Welsh Country Upbringing* by David Parry-Jones

Bara Brith

Bara Brith

Ingredients

450g mixed dried fruit

300ml cold tea, without milk

2 tablespoons marmalade

1 egg, beaten

6 tablespoons soft brown sugar

1 teaspoon mixed spice

450g self-raising flour

Honey, to glaze

Makes 1 loaf

Method

1 Soak the dried fruit overnight in the tea.

2 Next day, mix in the marmalade, egg, sugar, spice and flour.

3 Stir the mixture well and spoon into a 900g loaf tin.

4 Bake in a warm oven at 170°C/ 150°C Fan/Gas 4 for 1¾ hours, or until the centre is cooked through.

5 If the top is getting too brown, cover with some foil.

6 Once cooked, leave the bara brith to stand for 5 minutes, then tip out of the tin onto a cooling tray.

7 Using a pastry brush, glaze the top with runny honey.

8 Serve sliced with butter.

Bara brith literally means 'speckled bread' – a handful of dried fruit would be added to the last lump of dough at the end of a day's home baking to make a rich tea loaf. Originally made with a yeast dough, this modern recipe uses self-raising flour and is quick and easy to prepare.

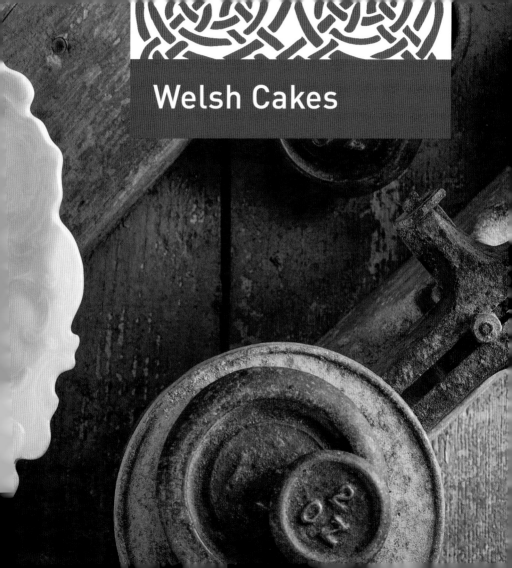

Welsh Cakes

Welsh Cakes

Ingredients

225g self-raising flour

100g butter

75g caster sugar

75g currants

½ teaspoon mixed spice

1 teaspoon runny honey

1 egg, beaten

Makes 15-18

Method

1 Rub the butter into the flour until it resembles breadcrumbs.

2 Add the caster sugar, currants, mixed spice, honey and beaten egg and stir until the mixture begins to stick together, then press to make a firm dough.

3 Roll or pat out on a floured board to a thickness of about 1cm and cut into rounds using a 6cm cutter.

4 Heat a frying pan or griddle to medium heat and dry griddle the Welsh cakes for about 3 minutes on each side.

5 Sprinkle with caster sugar as soon as you remove them from the pan.

Welsh cakes have been tea-time favourites in south Wales since the latter part of the 18th century. Moist and not too crumbly, miners would have expected to find them in their lunchboxes. Originally, they were cooked either on the griddle over the open fire or in what was known as a Dutch oven, a small metal container which was placed in front of the fire or in the warm ashes.

The Welsh names for Welsh cakes are *pice ar y maen* or *cacen gri*, which are based on the Welsh name for the griddle or bakestone.

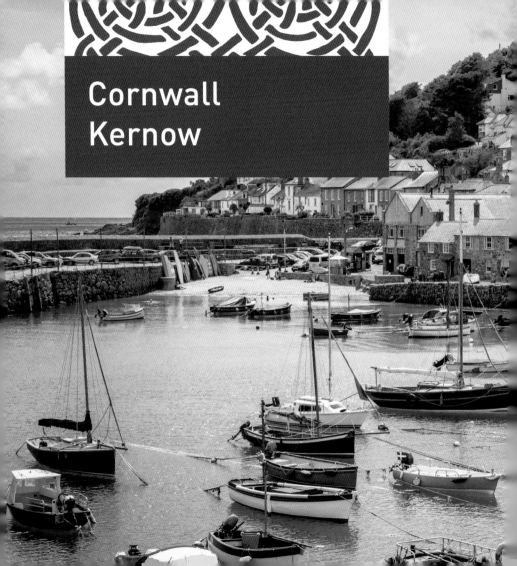

Cornwall
Kernow

Cornish Pasty

Cornish Pasty

Ingredients

For the pastry

500g strong bread flour

120g lard or white shortening, cubed

125g Cornish butter, cubed

1 teaspoon salt

175ml cold water

For the filling

400g good-quality beef skirt, cut into smallish cubes

300g waxy potatoes, peeled and diced

150g swede, peeled and diced

150g onion, peeled and sliced

Salt and pepper to taste

Beaten egg or milk, to glaze

Makes 6

Method

1 Add the salt to the flour in a large mixing bowl. Rub the two types of fat into the flour until the mixture resembles breadcrumbs.

2 Add the water, bring the mixture together with a round-bladed knife and knead until the pastry becomes elastic. This will take longer than normal pastry but it gives it the strength that is needed to hold the filling and retain a good shape.

3 Cover the pastry with cling film and leave to rest for 3 hours in the fridge.

4 Heat oven to 160°C/140°C Fan/ Gas 3.

5 Roll out the pastry on a floured surface and cut into circles 20cm in diameter.

6 Layer the vegetables and meat on top of the pastry, adding a generous pinch of salt and pepper as you go.

7 Bring the pastry around and crimp the edges together.

8 Glaze with beaten egg or an egg and milk mixture.

9 Bake for about 50-55 minutes until golden.

Few holiday makers visiting Cornwall will miss the opportunity to eat a delicious Cornish pasty.

Beef skirt is the cut traditionally used for Cornish pasties. This is the underside of the belly of the animal. It has no gristle and little fat, cooks in the same amount of time as the raw vegetables and its juice produces wonderful gravy.

Stargazy Pie

The dish is traditionally held to have originated from the village of Mousehole in Cornwall and is traditionally eaten during the festival of Tom Bawcock's Eve to celebrate his heroic catch during a very stormy winter. According to the modern festival, which is combined with the Mousehole village illuminations, the entire catch was baked into a huge stargazy pie, encompassing seven types of fish and saving the village from starvation.

Stargazy Pie

Ingredients

8 whole sardines

500g ready-made shortcrust pastry

200g onion, finely chopped

4 streaky bacon rashers, finely chopped

3 hard-boiled eggs, finely chopped

Salt and pepper to taste

1 lemon, juice only

1 egg, beaten

Serves 4

Method

1 Heat the oven to 200°C/180°C Fan/ Gas 6.

2 Roll out ⅔ of the pastry to cover the sides and base of a 20cm shallow pie dish. Brush the edges with milk.

3 Clean and bone the fish, leaving their heads in place. Season inside.

4 Lay the fish on the pastry like the spokes of a wheel with their heads on the rim.

5 Scatter the chopped onion, bacon and egg between the fish and season well. Squeeze over the lemon juice.

6 Roll out the remaining pastry and cover the top of the pie. Carefully cut slits into the pastry to reveal the heads of the fish.

7 Trim the excess pastry, then crimp the edges.

8 Brush the pie with beaten egg.

9 Cook for around 30 minutes until golden brown.

The pie is so called because the heads of the fish peep out through the pastry, gazing up to the sky.

Cornish Saffron
Cake

Cornish Saffron Cake

Ingredients

Good pinch saffron strands

125ml milk

500g plain flour

½ teaspoon dried, fast-action yeast

Pinch salt

Pinch nutmeg, freshly grated

250g cold butter, cut into cubes, plus extra for greasing

250g caster sugar

300g sultanas and currants, mixed

50g candied peel

Makes 1 loaf

Method

1 Line a 1kg loaf tin with baking parchment or grease well with butter.

2 Heat the saffron strands and milk in a pan over a medium heat until the milk mixture has turned yellow and is almost simmering. Leave to cool.

3 Rub the butter into the flour until the mixture resembles breadcrumbs. Add the yeast, salt, nutmeg, sugar and fruit and mix well.

4 Pour over the saffron-infused milk and stir until the mixture becomes a soft dough.

5 Turn the dough onto a lightly floured work surface and knead lightly until smooth.

6 Transfer the dough to the prepared loaf tin. Cover and set aside in a warm place for 30-45 minutes, or until risen.

7 Heat the oven to 180°C/160°C Fan/ Gas 4.

8 Bake the saffron cake for 45 minutes to 1 hour, or until it is pale golden brown and has risen.

9 Set the cake aside to cool slightly, then turn out of the loaf tin onto a plate and cut into slices. Serve well buttered.

The making of the legendary saffron cake is said to date back to the days when Phoenician traders exchanged spices and other goods for tin from the Cornish mines. The luxurious saffron spice, made from the dried stigmas of crocus flowers, was added to give exotic flavour to bread and cakes. The brilliant yellow colour of the saffron really brings appeal to the look of this cake.

Scones for a
Cornish Cream Tea

Scones for a Cornish Cream Tea

Cornwall is famous for serving the most delicious cream tea. The main ingredients are freshly baked and sometimes still warm scones, either fruit or plain, a really good fruit jam, often strawberry, with spoonfuls of clotted cream on top. And, of course, there is a pot of hot tea.

Ingredients

75g butter, cold

350g self-raising flour, plus extra for dusting

1 teaspoon baking powder

30g caster sugar

75g sultanas

100-150ml milk

2 eggs, beaten

To serve

Clotted or whipped cream

Good-quality jam, preferably strawberry

Makes 10

Method

1 Heat the oven to 220°C/200°C Fan/ Gas 7.

2 Put the flour and baking powder into a large mixing bowl and rub the flour in lightly and quickly with your fingertips until the mixture looks like fine breadcrumbs. Add the sugar and sultanas.

3 Pour 100ml of the milk and the beaten egg into the flour mixture.

4 Mix together with a round-bladed knife to a soft but not too sticky dough, adding a bit more milk if necessary.

5 Turn the dough out onto a lightly floured work surface, lightly knead just a few times, only until gathered together, then gently roll and pat out to about 2cm deep.

6 Cut out as many rounds as possible from the first rolling with a 6cm cutter and put them on the baking sheet, spaced slightly apart.

7 Press the trimmings together and then roll and cut out again. Repeat until you have 10 scones.

8 Brush the tops of the scones with a little milk and bake for about 10 minutes, or until risen and golden.

9 Remove and cool on a wire rack before splitting and adding the jam and cream.

To make plain scones, simply leave out the sultanas.

The secret to making scones is to do it quickly, working the dough as little as possible and cooking them straight away.

Cornish Ginger
Fairings

These biscuits were originally prepared for fairs around Britain and sold as edible treats to give to children or by men to give to their sweethearts.

Cornish Ginger Fairings

Ingredients

100g self-raising flour

1 lemon, rind only, finely grated

1 level teaspoon baking powder

1 level teaspoon ground ginger

1 level teaspoon mixed spice

1 level teaspoon ground cinnamon

Pinch bicarbonate of soda

50g butter

50g granulated sugar

2 tablespoons golden syrup

Makes about a dozen

Method

1 Heat the oven to 200°C/180°C Fan/Gas 6.

2 Mix all the dry ingredients together except for the granulated sugar.

3 Rub in the butter, then add the sugar.

4 Heat the syrup until it runs and add to the mixture.

5 Roll into balls the size of a walnut and place on a greased baking tray.

6 Bake on the top shelf of a fairly hot oven. When the biscuits begin to colour, remove to a lower shelf, where they will sink a bit and develop little cracks.

7 Cool the biscuits on a rack and store in a tin.

In Cornwall, fairings contained ginger
and became famous around the country
when a Cornish manufacturer started
selling them by mail order in 1886.
It is said that the original fairing was
two ginger biscuits and two sugared
almonds packaged by a lady in Truro.

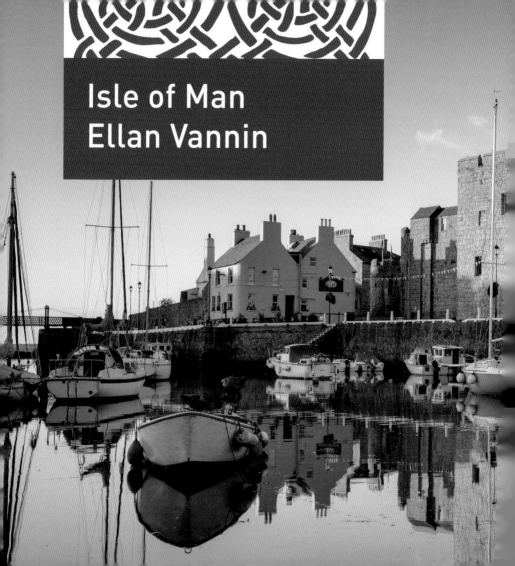

Isle of Man
Ellan Vannin

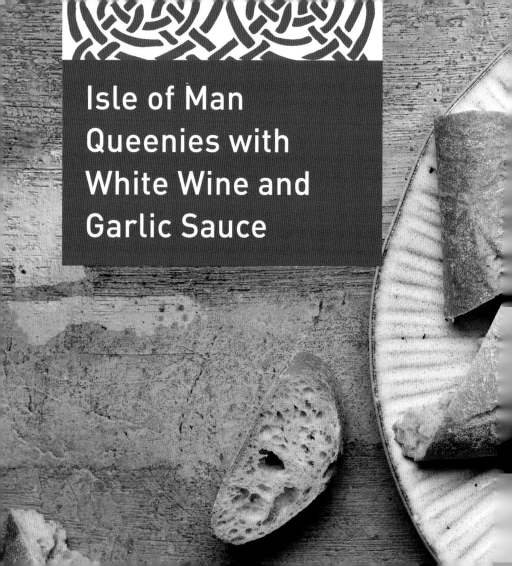

Isle of Man Queenies with White Wine and Garlic Sauce

Isle of Man Queenies with White Wine and Garlic Sauce

The queenie is a medium-sized species of scallop, growing to a maximum of 90mm in diameter, and the shell can vary in colour from yellow to orange, red, brown or purple. Fishing queenies has been a traditional industry on the Isle of Man since the mid-1800s, when they were used as bait in longline fishing for cod.

The Gulf Stream moderates the island's climate, which benefits from a warming temperature that provides temperate conditions. Summers tend to be cool and fairly sunny, while the winters are mild and wet with very little frost and snow.

Ingredients

500g queenie scallops

1 tablespoon olive oil

Salt and pepper

White wine and garlic sauce

25g butter

3 cloves garlic, peeled and finely chopped

100ml dry white wine

1 teaspoon lemon juice

2 tablespoons parsley, finely chopped

Salt and pepper to taste

Serves 4

Method

1 Heat a large non-stick frying pan over high heat.

2 Pat the scallops dry with paper towels. Toss lightly in olive oil and season with salt and pepper.

3 Add the scallops to the hot pan (do this in batches to avoid overcrowding the pan) and allow to panfry for 2-3 minutes per side until they are golden brown and seared on both sides.

4 Remove from the pan and keep warm.

5 Meanwhile, melt the butter in the pan then add the garlic. Allow to cook for 30 seconds, then pour in the white wine, lemon juice and parsley.

6 Bring the sauce to a simmer, then cook for 3-5 minutes until the sauce has reduced slightly.

7 Add the scallops back into the pan and allow to heat through.

8 Serve with chunks of crusty bread.

Isle of Man queenies can only be caught during the queenie season, which traditionally starts on 1 June.

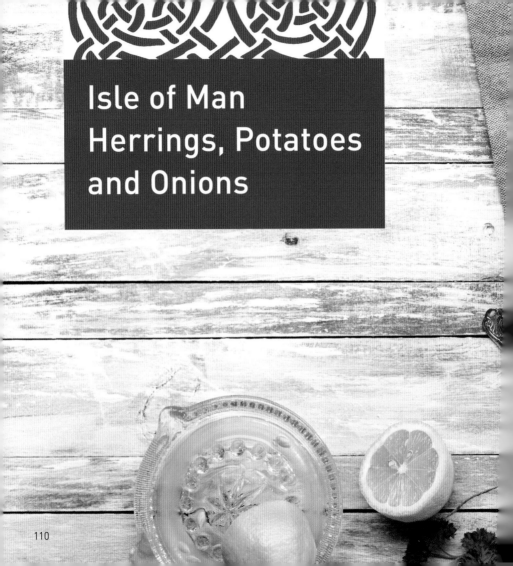

Isle of Man
Herrings, Potatoes
and Onions

Isle of Man Herrings, Potatoes and Onions

This dish is known as priddhas an' herrin', and as well as being the national dish of the Isle of Man, it is one of the simplest to prepare.

Consisting of herring, potatoes and raw onion, all three ingredients are Isle of Man staples and this dish would have supported the fishermen and farmers of the island. In the past most homes would have had a crockpot of salt herring kept by the back door or in the pantry. If you are using salt herring, you will need to soak them overnight in cold, fresh water to remove the salt.

Ingredients

2 herring per person, filleted

350g potatoes, peeled and cut into chunks

1 onion, peeled and sliced

Knobs of butter, to serve

Serves 4

Method

1 Heat the oven to 180°C/160°C Fan/ Gas 4.

2 Put the potatoes in a large saucepan and barely cover with water. Bring to the boil and cook for 5 minutes.

3 Transfer to a shallow baking tray.

4 Lay the herring fillets on top of the potatoes and bake in the oven for about 10-15 minutes, or until the fish and potatoes are cooked.

5 Serve with knobs of butter melted over the potatoes and slices of raw onion on top of the herring.

6 Enjoy with slices of crusty bread and a glass of buttermilk.

Bonnag – Manx Fruit Bread

Bonnag is a traditional Manx bread which has been around for hundreds of years.

Bonnag – Manx Fruit Bread

Ingredients

250g plain flour

100g sugar

100g currants

25g butter

1 teaspoon bicarbonate of soda

1 large teaspoon mixed spice

Few drops vanilla essence

100ml buttermilk, or fresh milk mixed with a teaspoon of fresh lemon juice

Makes 1 loaf

Method

1 Heat the oven to 180°C/160°C Fan/ Gas 4.

2 Put the flour into a large bowl and rub in the butter.

3 Add the other dry ingredients and stir to mix.

4 Pour in the vanilla essence and buttermilk to make a firm dough.

5 Shape into a large bun and put on a baking sheet.

6 Bake for around 1 hour until well risen and golden.

7 Serve sliced with butter.

Originally, as with other recipes from the Celtic countries, bonnag would have been a daily bread, a large, flat, unleavened loaf cooked on the griddle, rather like oatcakes, potato cakes, crêpes or Welsh cakes. Over the years it has become a much richer, cake-like fruit bread, baked in the oven.

Brittany
Breizh

Cotriade – Breton Fish Stew

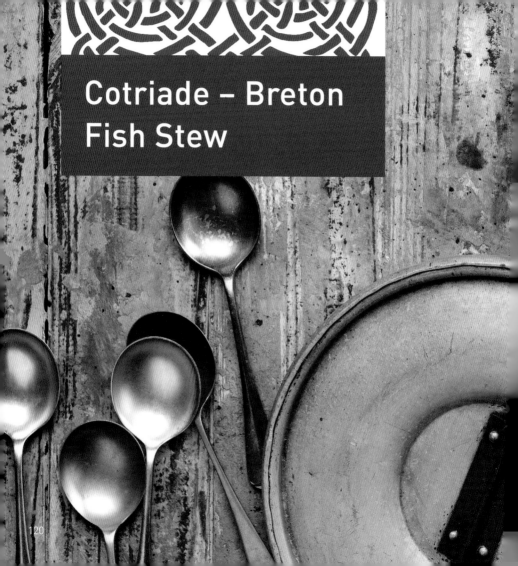

Cotriade – Breton Fish Stew

Ingredients

1kg selection of fish (mackerel, sardines, squid, ray, cod, etc.), trimmed and filleted

450g shellfish (langoustines, prawns, mussels), cleaned

1 tablespoon olive oil

Pinch saffron

3-4 cloves garlic, peeled and chopped

4 onions, peeled and sliced into rings

1kg potatoes, peeled and diced

6 tomatoes, peeled and diced

Small bunch parsley

1 stick celery, chopped

1 leek, chopped

1 bouquet garni

Seasoning

Serves 4-6

Method

1 Make some stock with all the fish trimmings. In a saucepan, cover with cold water, bring to the boil and simmer for 20 minutes, then strain to make 1½ litres.

2 Heat the olive oil in a large pan, add the saffron, garlic and onions and cook gently until soft.

3 Add the stock, potatoes, tomatoes, parsley, celery, leek and herbs. Season and cook until tender.

4 Add the firm fish to the pot first, layering up with the shellfish on top. Cook for about 5 minutes.

5 Serve the cotriade in large bowls with French bread and a good bottle of wine.

Almost every coastal region of France has their version of fish soup, and the Bretonnes call theirs 'cotriade'.

This is a recipe from Belle-Île, the largest and one of the best-known islands off the Brittany coast.

Galettes
Bretonnes

They are generally known in French as crêpes de blé noir, crêpes de sarrasin, or galettes de sarrasin, where galette means 'flat cake' and *blé noir* and *sarrasin* translate as buckwheat in English.

Galettes Bretonnes

Ingredients

Galette mixture

200g buckwheat flour

300ml milk

300ml water

1 egg, beaten

Pinch salt

50g unsalted butter, melted, plus additional for greasing the pan

Pinch ground nutmeg (optional)

Filling

6 eggs – 1 egg per galette

60g spinach, washed, chopped and squeezed dry

140g grated Gruyere or other hard cheese

Salt and black pepper

Makes 6

Method

1 Combine all the galette ingredients in a bowl and whisk until the batter is smooth. Leave in the fridge for at least an hour.

2 Gently heat a frying or galette pan and add a little butter.

3 Swirl a small ladleful of the galette mixture evenly over the pan, the thinner the better.

4 When the galette starts to set, crack the egg onto the middle of the batter.

5 Add the spinach and cheese so they surround the egg.

6 Leave the galette to cook on a medium to high heat until the egg starts to set. Season well.

7 Increase the heat to crisp up the galette and cook on a high heat for a few minutes until you see the sides start to brown.

8 When the galette is crisp, fold the sides into the middle, leaving the egg showing.

9 Serve immediately and repeat with the other 5 galettes.

Introduced in the 14th century and reaching its peak by the 19th century, buckwheat was grown in different regions of France with similar soil types, such as Limousin and Auvergne.

Nowadays, galettes bretonnes are made and eaten everywhere across France and beyond.

Poulet au Cidre

Poulet au Cidre

Ingredients

6 chicken breasts

2 apples, Golden Delicious variety, cut into cubes

3 large onions, peeled and sliced finely

50g butter

200ml dry cider from Brittany

2 tablespoons Calvados (optional)

2 pinches ground nutmeg

Salt and pepper to taste

50ml cream

Serves 6

Method

1 Melt half the butter in a large pan and cook the onions on medium heat for 5-7 minutes until golden.

2 In a larger, thicker pan, melt the remaining butter and brown the chicken breasts for about 3 minutes.

3 Add the cooked onions and apples and cover with the cider and cognac.

4 Add nutmeg, salt and pepper.

5 Allow to simmer without a lid until $2/3$ of the cider has evaporated, approximately 30-40 minutes.

6 Remove the chicken breasts and set aside to keep warm.

7 Pour the cream into the cider sauce and stir for a few minutes.

8 Coat the chicken with the sauce and serve immediately with rice or creamed potatoes.

This is a classic recipe from the north-east of France, where the apple harvest is plentiful and cider is the fashionable drink of the region.

Crêpe Bretonne

Crêpe Bretonne

Ingredients

150g plain flour

1 large egg, lightly beaten

375ml milk, approximately

50g butter

Fillings

1 lemon, squeezed juice and caster sugar

Or 60g jam of your favourite flavour and whipped cream

Or 250g strawberries, hulled and sliced and whipped cream

Or chocolate spread

Some icing sugar, for dusting

Makes 12 crêpes

Method

1 Sift the flour into a bowl and make a well in the centre. Add the egg and a little milk into the well, then gradually whisk in the flour, slowly adding more milk until you obtain a smooth, thin batter.

2 Strain the mixture through a fine sieve into a jug and stand for at least 10 minutes before cooking the crêpes.

3 Melt the butter in a 20cm crêpe pan, then whisk the hot, melted butter into the crêpe mixture.

4 To make the crêpes, pour enough mixture into the hot pan to thinly cover the base. Cook for 1 minute, or until the edges start to brown. Turn and cook the other side for 30 seconds, then transfer to a plate and repeat with the remaining batter, stacking the cooked crêpe as you go.

5 To assemble, spread each crepe with a little jam and cream and top with 4-5 slices of strawberry. Fold the crêpes and dust with icing sugar just before serving.

Brittany is regarded as the birthplace of these lovely, delicate pancakes, but you need to head to Lower Brittany, i.e. the regions of Finistere, part of Moribihan and Côte d'Amour, if you want to find an authentic sweet crêpe made from wheat flour.

Although fresh lemon juice and sugar is a particular favourite, you can fill the crêpes with almost anything, but make sure you rest the batter prior to cooking, as this allows the gluten to relax and makes for a tender, delicate pancake.

Pain d'Epices

This is a traditional recipe from Brittany which translates to 'bread of spices'.

Pain d'Epices

Ingredients

4 level tablespoons runny honey

150ml boiling water

225g plain flour

Pinch salt

100g caster sugar

1 teaspoon mixed spice

1 teaspoon ground ginger

1 level teaspoon bicarbonate of soda

1 level teaspoon baking powder

Makes 1 loaf

Method

1. Heat the oven to 180°C/160°C Fan/ Gas 4.

2. Oil and flour or line a 900g loaf tin.

3. Stir the honey into the boiling water and leave to cool.

4. Sieve the flour with the salt and add the sugar and spice.

5. Using a wooden spoon, add the melted honey and water, beating until bubbles appear.

6. Stir in the baking powder and bicarbonate of soda.

7. Pour the mixture into the loaf tin and bake for an hour, or until a skewer inserted into the loaf comes out clean with no trace of dough left on it.

8. Serve the loaf warm or cold, as it is or spread with butter or cream cheese.

It is very similar to Welsh spiced honey loaf and a family favourite, particularly good to ward off hunger when on a beach along the Brittany coast during the long days of summer.

Galicia
Galiza

Caldo Gallego

A Galician peasant soup originally made from root crops and dried beans, this hearty soup now incorporates meat and is found all over Spain.

Caldo Gallego

Ingredients

1 tablespoon olive oil

1 medium onion, diced

1 clove garlic, finely chopped

100g chorizo, sliced

100g smoked ham, diced

1 medium potato, peeled and diced

2 medium turnips or parsnips, peeled and diced

1 litre vegetable stock

1 x 400g can white cannellini beans

2 cups chopped greens, such as kale, chard or dark leaf

Serves 4-6

Method

1 Heat the oil in a large saucepan over medium heat.

2 Add the onion and sauté for 5 minutes then add the garlic and cook for another minute.

3 Stir in the chorizo and ham and cook until lightly browned.

4 Add the potatoes and turnips, then pour in stock and bring to a boil. Cover and simmer gently until the potatoes and turnips are tender, about 20 minutes.

5 Stir in the beans and greens and cook until the greens are tender, at least 3 minutes.

Traditionally a filling and warming dish to help strengthen agricultural workers against the colder weather, each village, town or even household in Galicia would make different varieties based on the ingredients they could get their hands on. You can still expect to find distinctive versions wherever you go in the region today.

Empanada
Gallega

With a history dating back to the 7th century, this empanada Gallega has been supporting pilgrims throughout their travels along the Camino de Santiago.

Empanada Gallega

Ingredients

1 tablespoon olive oil

1 onion, finely chopped

1 clove garlic, crushed

3 medium potatoes, peeled and diced

2 carrots, peeled and diced

2 red peppers, seeded and diced

1 tablespoon smoked paprika

1 teaspoon each dried oregano and thyme

2 tablespoons tomato purée

300ml vegetable stock

1 x 185g can tuna in brine, flaked

500g pack shortcrust pastry

1 egg, beaten

Serves 6

Method

1 Heat the oven to 200°C/180°C Fan/Gas 6.

2 Heat the oil in a large frying pan and cook the onion, garlic, potatoes and carrots for 5 minutes until softening.

3 Add the peppers, paprika, herbs and tomato purée and cook for another 5 minutes.

4 Add the stock, bring to the boil, then simmer until the stock is absorbed and the vegetables are tender.

5 Stir in the tuna and leave to cool.

6 Roll a quarter of the pastry into a 22cm circle. Roll the remaining pastry to line a 22cm loose-bottomed tin, allowing the pastry to come over the edges of the tin.

7 Fill with the tuna mix and top with the pie lid.

8 Brush the edges with beaten egg, then fold over the sides and press down with a fork to seal.

9 Make two holes in the top, brush with the egg and bake for 35-40 minutes until golden brown.

10 Leave to cool slightly, then serve.

With a tasty filling and firm pastry crust, this makes the ideal food for travellers and has many similarities to the Cornish pasty.

Tarta de Santiago

Originating from Galicia during the time of medieval pilgrimage, this moist orange cake is traditionally decorated with the St James cross outlined on the top in icing sugar.

Tarta de Santiago

Ingredients

2 oranges, total weight 280g, scrubbed and roughly chopped, skins on

5 eggs, separated

200g caster sugar

225g ground almonds

2 tablespoons flaked almonds

Sifted icing sugar, to decorate

Serves 6-8

Method

1 Put the chopped oranges in a small saucepan, discarding any pips. Add 1 tablespoon water, then cover and cook gently for 30 minutes or until the oranges are soft and excess liquid has evaporated. Leave to cool.

2 Heat the oven to 180°C/160°C Fan/ Gas 4.

3 Line the bottom and sides of a 23cm springform cake tin with baking parchment.

4 Finely chop the oranges in a food processor, blender, or with a large knife.

5 Whisk the egg whites in a large bowl until they form stiff peaks. Gradually whisk in the caster sugar, little by little, alternating with the egg yolks until you have a thick mousse.

6 Gently fold in the finely chopped oranges and the ground almonds.

7 Transfer the mixture to the prepared tin and level the top. Sprinkle with the flaked almonds.

8 Bake for 45-50 minutes, or until the cake is golden and a skewer inserted in the centre comes out clean. Cover lightly with foil if it is browning too quickly.

9 Leave the cake to cool in the tin before turning out.

Recipe notes

Recipe notes

Gilli Davies

Gilli Davies is a food writer and Cordon Bleu chef from Wales. As an author, Gilli has written a total of twelve books on the food of Wales, Cyprus and organic produce and has been involved with food, food journalism and broadcasting since about 1980.

In 2011 Graffeg published Gilli's *Flavours of Wales* recipe book, ideal for those who enjoy simple home-cooked dishes and flavours. *Flavours of Wales* is also available as a small pocket guide, part of the Pocket Wales collection, and full recipes are included on the *Flavours of Wales* notecards.

The *Flavours of Wales Collection* cookbook was published in October 2015, followed by a series of compact Flavours of Wales titles covering baking, cheese, seasalt, seaweed, Welsh lamb and Welsh cakes during 2016 and 2017.

Gilli went on to publish 12 Flavours of England cookbooks through 2019 and 2020, celebrating the best of English cuisine, including the classic English breakfast, pies and pasties, afternoon tea and vegetarian dishes.

Metric and imperial equivalents

Weights	Solid
15g	½oz
25g	1oz
40g	1½oz
50g	1¾oz
75g	2¾oz
100g	3½oz
125g	4½oz
150g	5½oz
175g	6oz
200g	7oz
250g	9oz
300g	10½oz
400g	14oz
500g	1lb 2oz
1kg	2lb 4oz
1.5kg	3lb 5oz
2kg	4lb 8oz
3kg	6lb 8oz

Volume	Liquid
15ml	½ floz
30ml	1 floz
50ml	2 floz
100ml	3½ floz
125ml	4 floz
150ml	5 floz (¼ pint)
200ml	7 floz
250ml	9 floz
300ml	10 floz (½ pint)
400ml	14 floz
450ml	16 floz
500ml	18 floz
600ml	1 pint (20 floz)
1 litre	1¾ pints
1.2 litre	2 pints
1.5 litre	2¾ pints
2 litres	3½ pints
3 litres	5¼ pints